Table of Contents

Dedication: 4
Acknowledgements: 5
Introduction 6
Chapter 1 — Signs Before the Time Has Come 8
Chapter 2 — The 2 Witnesses 25
Chapter 3 — The End Time Church 61
Chapter 4 — The 144,000 77
Closing Thoughts 86
I'd love to hear from you 87
Other books by Matthew Robert Payne 88
About the Author 89

Dedication:

I dedicate this work to the Holy Spirit. Through his guidance and love, I had the courage to release this project. I hope that the Holy Spirit confirms these words in the hearts of people.

Optimistic Visions of Revelation

The End Times Church, Signs of the Times,
The Two Witnesses and the 144,000

Matthew Robert Payne

This book is copyrighted © by Matthew Robert Payne 2016.

All Scripture is taken from the New King James Version (NKJV) unless otherwise indicated. Copyright © 1982 by Thomas Nelson, Inc. Used by permission. All rights reserved.

Scripture quotations marked New Living Translation (NLT) are taken from the Holy Bible, New Living Translation, copyright © 1996, 2004, 2007 by Tyndale House Foundation. Used by permission of Tyndale House Publishers, Inc., Carol Stream, Illinois 60188. All rights reserved.

You can sow into Matthew's ministry, read his blog, view his published books or request your own personal prophecy or life coaching at http://personal-prophecy-today.com.

Cover design by Akira007 from Fiverr.com
Editing by Lisa Thompson at writebylisa.com

The opinions expressed by the author are not necessarily those of Revival Waves of Glory Books & Publishing.

Published by Revival Waves of Glory Books & Publishing
PO Box 596| Litchfield, Illinois 62056 USA
www.revivalwavesofgloryministries.com

Revival Waves of Glory Books & Publishing is committed to excellence in the publishing industry.

Book design Copyright © 2016 by Revival Waves of Glory Books & Publishing. All rights reserved.

Published in the United States of America

Paperback: 978-1-63227-140-2
Hardcover: 978-1-68411-109-1

Acknowledgements:

Revival Waves of Glory Books and Publishing:

I want to thank Bill Vincent for producing this book for me and doing all of the heavy lifting.

Lisa Thompson:

I want to thank my editor for all of the work that she has done to prepare this book to be published.

My mother:

I want to thank my mother for being there for me to talk to as I worked on this book. Each book has its own pressures and reasons why I might become stressed, and this book was no different.

The workers at Fiverr:

I want to thank the designer at Fiverr for this cover and the typist that faithfully typed up this manuscript. I don't know what I would do without Fiverr.

The readers:

I want to thank the readers of this book for motivating me to write it. It was with you in mind that I tried my best to make the following scenarios understandable. I pray that you will be at ease as you read this information.

Introduction

The book of Revelation is a complex book, one that has been very hard for people to understand and unravel. This book will not address everything that is covered in Revelation. However, I will briefly cover some of the signs of the times, information about the two witnesses, the end time church as I see her, and the 144,000 servants.

My opinion of these signs that need to happen before Christ returns is not an exhaustive list nor is it covered with the expertise that a theologian would bring to such a subject. I am just a lay person with no theological experience who is simply sharing as best as I can.

When I cover the role of the two witnesses, my perspective is not meant to be factual and does not address the actual events as they might unfold. I just wanted to paint a possible yet detailed picture of what the two witnesses might do. I have read scores of accounts by people about the two witnesses, but none of them that I read went into any detail of the activities of the two witnesses. This account appeared to me in something similar to a vision. I hope that as you read it that you will form an idea of the massive impact that the two witnesses will have when they come to earth. Once again, I want people to know that the plagues and judgments mentioned in this part of the book are simply my ponderings of the sort of things that the prophets will do and are **not** the exact plagues that will occur.

When I cover the end time church, I hope in my heart that the picture I paint will be fairly close to what will happen in the last days before Christ returns. I don't often discuss the book of Revelation with other Christians, yet one time when I shared this vision I had of the end time church with a friend, she was able to confirm that she had heard similar accounts from popular speakers in the church. I personally believe that a certain number of Christians will escape the antichrist and the mark of the beast as alluded to in Revelation 12:14-16, and this book expands on my views.

I have had a number of visions of the 144,000 and have pondered their roles quite a bit as I feel that I am one of them. I have fleshed out my beliefs about the 144,000 in that section. Of course, people might object to some or all of what I say about them, so I guess this book is for the people with open minds.

I want to stress that I called this book "Optimistic Visions of Revelation" so that I would not be dogmatic and assume that things are going to play out exactly like I have covered. I chose the title as it is a hopeful vision that I have of the most misunderstood book of the Bible.

I stand first in line to be corrected and humbly write this to inspire some of you. Rather than saying that this book is 100 percent accurate, I put this future to you as something that I hope for instead of the scary beliefs that are commonly shared on the book of Revelation.

Chapter 1 — Signs Before the Time Has Come

Many Christians read material about the book of Revelation by famous teachers. Some of those saints believe in a pre-tribulation rapture, a time when God snatches the people of God away from the earth before a great tribulation.

The people who believe this might not be prepared for suffering and trials that might come during the tribulation period that is mentioned in the Bible. I feel that someone had to write a book that at least touches on this topic. Many people assume that they're going to be snatched away at any time and that God is going to come and rescue them and take them away.

I feel that people who believe in a pre-tribulation rapture need to read other books with different views. One good book that agrees with what I believe is called "The Rapture Verdict" by Michael Snyder (2016), and you can order yourself a copy, which has a whole lot more Scriptures than this small book of mine. It presents a solid biblical argument for when the rapture will happen.

First, I want to start with a personal story to underscore why I don't believe that Jesus is coming to earth any time soon.

My Vision of the Books

A couple of years ago, I had a vision of heaven and met Jesus there. He showed me a bookcase with a number of books. I heard the number "50" in my spirit, so I assumed that the bookcase held 50 books. At that time, I had written about eight books, and Jesus told me that the bookcase was full of books that I was going to write in my life.

As I said, I had only written about eight books at the time. This was quite a surprise to me. Writing 50 books — especially if you have only written eight books — is a ton of work. It takes a lot of time, money, energy and resources to produce that many books. I also knew that I would have to acquire a lot of knowledge to publish 50 books.

I was surprised, but Jesus assured me that I was going to write those 50 books. When I was there in the vision, I tried to lean in and look at the titles of some of the books to get an idea of what the books were about, but I wasn't able to read the book titles. I felt Jesus laugh at my tenacity to try to find out the subjects.

About six months, later I had a dream. I saw about 30 orange golf balls and about 20 yellow golf balls, a total of 50 golf balls. They were just sitting beside the green of a golf course in a pile in mud. I found a plastic bag and collected them all and took them home.

I posted the dream on a dream interpretation Facebook page, and the person who interpreted the dream was a friend of mine, Sheldon. He explained that the 50 golf balls represented 50 books that I was going to write. They showed what I was going to do with the rest of my life.

I understand that I have 50 books to write. In the last year, I produced about eight books, bringing my total to 18 published books. At the rate of eight books a year, it will still take me six years to write 50 books.

Personally, that tells me that Jesus isn't coming back any time soon. I have a suspicion that Jesus showed me 50 books so that I would think about and focus on becoming an author and on writing books as a major assignment in my life. I have a sense that I'm going to write even more books, and that number could easily increase to 60 or even 80 books. I think that perhaps Jesus will show me even more books in the bookcase and just update that number when I've written 30 or 40 books.

That vision tells me that Jesus isn't coming back in 2016 or even 2017. He wouldn't show me a vision of 50 books if I wasn't going to actually write those books.

Confirmation from an Apostle in India

Here is another personal story that I heard from an Indian apostle who pastors a church there. Every year on his birthday, this man has a unique experience. Jesus comes down in the flesh, meets with him and talks to him.

This man was led to the Lord and saved by Jesus himself. Jesus appeared to him in the flesh as he was a reading a Bible, trying to understand what Jesus was teaching in the Gospels. Jesus told him that he was the man in the book and asked him what he wanted to know. Jesus led him to himself and baptized the man in water and in fire.

For 40 days, the man actually had to sleep in a well where it was cool because his skin was burning with the fire of God. Anyway, this man meets with Jesus once a year and has a strong relationship with him. He made a promise to Jesus that he would plant 1,500 churches. Like any promise you make with God, it's a two-way covenant that you make with your Creator.

This man agreed to plant 1,500 churches in India. So far, he has planted about 450 of the churches. He has a Bible college, but he needs people to go to new villages and plant churches. His church numbers are slowly growing each year.

Sadly enough, in India, they need finances. They need people in the West to support them. The work would grow a lot more quickly if he had more money to use.

He's a man who's promised to plant 1,500 churches. Jesus has never come down and adjusted that figure but has kept the number at 1,500. This man is producing new churches and planting them as fast as he can and is going to do his best to work toward the goal that he's set and the promise that he's made to Jesus.

This man has been saved and in ministry for 20 years and has planted 450 churches in that time. He might be increasing in how quickly the churches are planted in his country, yet he's not going to plant another 1,050 churches in the next couple of years.

Once again, this is a personal story that I'm aware of that shows that Jesus isn't coming back any time soon. You might have your own personal stories if you stop to think about it. You might have had prophecies spoken over your life and the future that have not happened yet for you. If so, you need to wait until they are fulfilled.

I want to now share a few Scriptures with you that are signs before the time has come.

The first scripture is Habakkuk 2:14. It reads, "For the Earth will be filled with the knowledge of the glory of the Lord, as the waters cover the sea."

We know that waters cover the sea, and the sea consists of the waters in the ocean. Just as the sea is made up of water, the whole world is going to be aware and have the knowledge of the glory of the Lord. The glory of the Lord manifests in signs, wonders and miracles. The glory of the Lord manifests on people's skin as light, and it manifests in the presence of peace in the joy of the Lord.

When that glory manifests, the people of the world are going to come to realize that there's a real God who displays his true glory. They will see that signs and wonders happen in Christian circles with specific miracles that happen in God's presence and in his glory.

The average person will come to the knowledge of God's glory in the world. They're going to personally experience his glory.

Many Christians at this time, including myself, don't have any idea of what the glory of the Lord actually is.

I know that the glory can manifest in gold dust, feathers, gemstones, multiplication of food, multiplication of money, sudden finances and bank accounts with unexplainable funds. These are all different signs of the glory of the Lord Jesus Christ.

Like me, many Christians don't know what the glory of the Lord really looks like. I am aware that some people do minister in the glory realms and do write books about the glory.

These people have a better idea about the glory realms and about what happens in the glory. All I know is that many Christians have no idea what the glory is, yet the Word tells us that in the future, everyone will understand what the glory of the Lord is.

Everyone will have a knowledge of the glory of the Lord as it is manifested. This must happen before Jesus Christ comes back to earth. The glory should be present and acknowledged and believed in before Jesus Christ returns.

Isaiah 60:1-3 says, "Arise, shine, for your light has come and the glory of the Lord is risen upon you. For behold, the darkness shall cover the earth, and deep darkness the people; but the Lord will arise over you, and His glory will be seen upon you. The Gentiles shall come to your light and kings to the brightness of your rising."

Isaiah prophesied here that at a certain time in the world, the glory of the Lord would appear on those people who are following the Lord.

When God's glory appears on a person, their skin shines. Sometimes, you might look at a Christian person and see that they are a really beautiful person. You will have the feeling that they're full of light, and you will see a manifestation on the person that shows how loving they are. This light shines on the person and can be seen visibly on his or her skin as it shines with the glory of the Lord.

This prophecy in Isaiah says that the glory of the Lord will arise upon certain people. I feel that in the future, people will manifest the glory of the Lord. That glory can actually shine as a light on a person.

My Experience with the Glory

I was once walking through Brisbane, a northern city in Australia. As I was strolling through the city, people were staring at me. Everyone that I passed seemed to look at me rudely. Sometimes, people just glance at you and then look away, but other times, people keep on staring at you. On this day, a lot of people kept looking at me.

Some people came up to me and asked me for the time. I wasn't wearing a watch, and this happened long before cell phones were in common use. I told them that I didn't know the time. Some people approached me and asked me if I had a light for their cigarettes. It seemed that everyone was interested in me. Some people were so interested that they made any excuse to come and talk to me.

The people that were asking me for the time and the people that asked me for a light for their cigarette were people that had seen something in me that they liked. They simply wanted some type of interaction with me.

I went to a bathroom in the city mall. I looked in the mirror to see if there was anything on my face or if I could see anything wrong with myself. Did I have green hair, or did I have a mark on my face, or could I see why people were looking at me?

I couldn't find anything. I spent the whole day in the city, and later that night, I was listening to a busker — a street musician —

as he was playing his music. This youth came along. He started talking to me. "What is it about you?"

I answered, "What do you mean?"

He asked, "What do you believe in?"

I replied, "I believe in Jesus Christ. I'm a Christian."

He responded, "I'm a Christian, too. But what do you believe?"

I told him, "I believe in Jesus Christ. I'm also baptized in the Holy Spirit. That might be the difference."

He stated, "I'm baptized in the Holy Spirit, too, but what is it about you?"

I wanted to listen to the busker. I was getting frustrated with this young person. I raised my voice. "What is **it** about me?"

He observed, "Your face is glowing. It looks like you've got a torch under your skin. Your whole face is shining brightly. I want to know what you're into. What do you believe in? Why are you like this?"

I was surprised. I had never seen that before and had never heard of anyone's face shining like the sun. This happened at night, so my skin must have been shining brightly for him to be able to see it glow. That incident really surprised me. I came to realize that when my face was shining like that, people reacted.

Another time, I was at a shopping center a few years later. People were looking at me again. I went up to this certain take-away store. As soon as I approached the counter, a lady serving asked me, "What is your order?"

A line of people were waiting at the store. I knew that some of the people in the line hadn't been served. I told her, "You might want to serve these other people first. I can wait."

When I said that, the people turned around and looked at me. They probably saw my face shining, too.

I realized that if your face shines like this, I will have favor with people, which opens up opportunities to share Jesus and his love with other people. This has happened to me about four or five times in my life so far. It's just a manifestation of the glory that rests upon me at certain times.

Isaiah 60:3 says, "The Gentiles will come to your light and kings to the brightness of your rising."

Verse 5 says, "Then you shall see and become radiant and your heart shall swell with joy because the abundance of the sea shall be turned to you, the wealth of the Gentiles shall come to you."

This Scripture seems to support the belief that people who recognize the glory that is on your life will show up with offerings and bring you wealth.

You might be in a business, or you might be in the ministry. The glory of the Lord might come upon that ministry. It will provoke and encourage people to take stock of their finances and deliver some of their funds to you because of the glory that's on your life.

This is one of the signs that is going to happen before the return of Jesus.

The next verse I want to share is 2 Thessalonians 2:3. "Let no one deceive you by any means: for that Day will not come unless the falling away comes first and the man of sin is revealed, the son of perdition, who opposes and exalts himself above all that is called God or that is worshipped, so that he sits as God in the temple of God, showing himself that he is God."

Many people who believe in a pre-tribulation rapture actually think that they're going to escape earth. They imagine that they're going to leave earth before the antichrist actually comes. They believe that the Christians who are living on the earth will be called by God and disappear before any problems come. This verse tends to say something different.

It says, "let no one deceive you by any means: for that Day will not come unless the falling away comes first and the man of sin is revealed, the son of perdition." It's very clear that the antichrist is going to come to earth before the day of the Lord.

Many people will take issue with that and argue, "That's not true. I don't believe that."

This is one of the reasons why Paul said, "Don't let anyone deceive you." It stands to reason that Paul knew that people were going to be deceived and that they were going to believe something that wasn't true.

He wanted to stress that it's not true that you are going disappear before the man of sin arrives, before the antichrist arrives. It's not true that we are going to leave earth before the antichrist comes. What is true is that there will be a great falling away of people, and the antichrist will come.

Many people wonder what will cause this great falling away. Why would people leave the faith?

One of the reasons for this that Michael shares in "The Rapture Verdict" is that many people have been taught that they're not going to go through tribulation and suffering before Jesus returns. They might be disappointed by the difficulties they face and fall away.

Many people might give up their faith at that time. They will have thought that they were being deceived and lied to by their pastors who preached the pre-tribulation rapture to them. That is why Paul says, "Don't let anyone deceive you." He wouldn't be writing that under the inspiration of the Holy Spirit if people were not able to be deceived. These people that were deceived or misled or told things that weren't actually true might walk away from the faith and give up.

Many believe that the antichrist might round up people who refuse to take the mark of the beast and take them to be killed. These people might deny their faith at this time. Preachers in those days will say that you can take the mark and still go to heaven due to the grace of God.

The rapture might not come when people expect it to come, so they might find themselves going through really harsh and trying times. Their faith might fail. They might leave the Christian faith behind, turn their backs on it and go back to the world.

People might fall away for a number of reasons. They might not even deal with any pressure; some people lose a loved one and become offended with God. They turn away and go back to the world. However, this verse tends to concentrate on a **great** falling away. It seems that many Christians have turned away and started to walk **contrary** to the faith of God. The Christian church will understand this concept.

According to this passage, it looks like Jesus won't return until first, the falling away happens, and second, the antichrist has appeared. Otherwise, Paul was wrong to write this, and we've got an error in Scripture. I might also humbly say that I could be wrong for interpreting this Scripture this way.

Many people place the rapture before the tribulation, which would be before the first of the seven trumpets that blow. If you believe that the tribulation happens after the rapture, then this verse certainly wouldn't make sense to you.

I Corinthians 15:52, 53 tells us, "In a moment, in the twinkling of an eye, at the last trumpet. For the trumpet will sound, and the dead will be raised incorruptible and we shall be changed. For this corruptible must put on incorruption, and this mortal must put on immortality."

It says that "in a twinkling of an eye at the last trumpet. For the trumpet will sound, and the dead will be raised incorruptible"

This verse says that the dead in Christ will rise again at the last trumpet — not at the first trumpet, not before the first trumpet, but at the last trumpet.

If you know Scripture, you might understand that at the end of the testimony of the two witnesses, the last trumpet blew in Revelation. This happens when the two witnesses leave the earth. This verse confirms that "the dead shall be raised at the last trumpet."

Once again, the last trumpet is the last trumpet; it's not the first trumpet, and it's not before the first trumpet. This verse points toward people staying a little bit longer.

One Scripture that is poignant for this time and as a sign is 2 Timothy 3:7, "Always learning and never able to come to the knowledge of the truth."

Many people live a Christian life, and they seem to go to church hundreds of times in their lives. They might read book after book or listen to YouTube video after YouTube video. They are very involved in the Christian life. This Scripture says that they're always learning and never able to come to the knowledge of the truth.

Let me share two teachings in the Bible that have been heard but that people have not understood. John expressed one of these truths, and even James and the other apostles backed him up.

1 John 2:15-17 says in the New Living Translation, "Do not love this world nor the things it offers you, for when you love the world, you do not have the love of the Father in you. For the world offers only a craving for physical pleasure, a craving for everything we see, and pride in our achievements and possessions. These are not from the Father, but are from this world. And this world is fading away, along with everything that people crave. But anyone who does what pleases God will live forever."

First of all, we can see the final phrase, "but anyone who does what pleases God will live forever." He says this to illustrate the point that anyone who loves the world isn't pleasing to God.

John tells us not to love the world or the things that it offers you because if you love the world, the love of the Father is not in you.

Despite regular "Christian" activity, many Christians still do not understand that Jesus does not want them to become a part of this world or to love this world. Jesus and the Father want people to be totally set apart and holy, to be in the world but not of it.

That means living a life that's separate and living a life that's extraordinarily different than the average person who lives in this world. John instructs us to not crave physical pleasure, crave everything we see or have pride in our achievements or in our possessions.

This is the lust of the eyes, the lust of the flesh and the pride of life in this passage. Many people I know don't understand how to live a life that is set apart for God. They don't know how to live a life where their focus is on God and his Kingdom or on loving their neighbors as they love themselves.

Many people spend a lot of much money on possessions, status, looking good and keeping up with the Jones'. They don't set aside money for the poor or for God's Kingdom. Their focus is on appearing good before men. Their focus isn't on loving God with all of their heart, mind and soul and loving their neighbors as themselves.

Many people are learning but never coming to the knowledge of the truth.

An amazing amount of Christians in the first world live a life of luxury compared to the third world. They live a life of extravagance, and they don't live holy and set apart lives.

Revelation 3:15-17 reads as follows: "I know your works, that you are neither cold nor hot. I could wish you were cold or hot. So then, because you are lukewarm, and neither cold nor hot, I will vomit you out of My mouth. Because you say, 'I am rich, have become wealthy, and have need of nothing'—and do not know that you are wretched, miserable, poor, blind, and naked"

This verse is sadly true of so many people in the church who don't feel that they need God because they are rich in the world's goods and follow in the world's ways.

Paul was saying to Timothy that these people are always learning and never coming to the knowledge of the truth. The truth is that you need to live a life that is set apart and holy. Holy isn't just living a life that's free from sin, which it should include, but it's much more. It's living a life that's consecrated and set apart for Jesus.

People seem ignorant of several truths in the Word. They might not know that Jesus had upwards of 50 commands in the Bible or 50 ways that he said to obey to him.

John 14:21, "He who has My commandments and keeps them, it is he who loves Me. And he who loves Me will be loved by My Father, and I will love him and manifest Myself to him."

Are you always learning and never able to come to the knowledge of the truth? Jesus says, "The person who loves me is the person who obeys my commandments."

I find that that over 90 percent of Christians have no idea what the commandments of Jesus are. You can look on Google and type in "The 50 commands of Jesus," and you'll find an article that lists 50 commandments of Jesus. Scripture references tell where each of them can be found. Jesus says quite clearly, "He who has my commandments and keeps them is he who loves me."

Jesus just shared about how to live the proper Christian life in the Sermon on the Mount. He gave what many consider to be the best speech in human history. He included many of the commands to his people in the Sermon on the Mount.

Then Jesus finished in Matthew 7:26-27, "But everyone who hears these sayings of Mine, and does not do them, will be like a foolish man who built his house on the sand: and the rain descended, the floods came, and the winds blew and beat on that house; and it fell. And great was its fall."

Jesus is saying that people who don't obey his commands are like the foolish builder who built their house upon the sand. Speaking of Revelation and of trying times, you could call what the world is going to enter into during the days of Revelation and the judgments a great flood or a great rain.

I'd encourage you to look up the 50 commands of Jesus and start to obey and walk in them. Begin to live a life of love for God and your fellow men as Jesus taught rather than being called a "Christian," which means "Christ follower." Perhaps you can change and become a disciple of Christ, someone who follows what he taught and who walks in his footsteps.

These are just two areas where are people are always learning but never able to come to the knowledge of the truth. People need to be set apart, live a life separate from the world and come out from the world and be holy. People need to understand the 50 commands of Jesus and obey them.

2 Timothy 4:3 says, "For the time will come when they will not endure sound doctrine, but according to their own desires, because they have itching ears, they will heap up for themselves teachers"

A popular teaching out there at the moment claims that Jesus was teaching the law on steroids. Some grace teachers believe that you don't have to obey what Jesus taught. John 14:21-23 says,

> " 'He who has My commandments and keeps them, it is he who loves Me. And he who loves Me will be loved by My Father, and I will love him and manifest Myself to him.' Judas (not Iscariot) said to Him, 'Lord, how is it that You will manifest Yourself to us, and not to the world?' Jesus answered and said to him, 'If anyone loves Me, he will keep My word; and My Father will love him, and We will come to him and make Our home with him.' "

If Jesus taught people to obey him and his commands, then we should follow him. Jesus says quite clearly that people that don't love him don't obey his commands.

The apostle John tells us in his letter, 1 John 2:4-6: "He who says, 'I know Him,' and does not keep His commandments, is a liar, and the truth is not in him. But whoever keeps His word, truly the love of God is perfected in him. By this we know that we are in Him. He who says he abides in Him ought himself also to walk just as He walked."

John is saying that if you say that you know Jesus but don't keep his commands, then you are a liar, and the truth isn't in you. Not only are people not being taught that they need to obey the commands of Jesus, but some grace teachers are preaching that you can intentionally ignore these commands because Jesus was teaching the law.

The church has elevated teachers who make them happy because they preach that you don't have to obey Jesus. Many teachers will come into the world who teach on subjects that are easy to comprehend and easy to accept — teachers who simply please the listeners.

People will be attracted to the belief that they will escape the world before the tribulation. This popular teaching attracts the people of the world because they think they won't have to suffer or endure the tribulation.

Once again, I believe this teaching is in error. People believe it in these last days, and teachers are not sharing the truth. Some Christians just want an easy life, so they follow these teachers.

A harmful doctrine is going around now that says that since Jesus died for everyone's sins, everyone is going to heaven. Even satan and the demons will be restored to Jesus. Everyone will end up happy, and no one will go to hell, which doesn't actually exist.

Thousands of people believe these lies. They are being swept up and believe that Jesus died for everyone's sins, and they believe that even those who don't choose to believe in Jesus will still be saved.

Many of these dangerous doctrines that are being taught will increase as the time draws closer to the end. Strange teachings will arise, and people will use multiple Bible verses taken out of context and be very convincing with their words.

The apostle Paul commands Timothy to preach and to share the Word in 2 Timothy 4:2. "Preach the word! Be ready in season and out of season. Convince, rebuke, exhort, with all longsuffering and teaching."

Previously, he observed in 2 Timothy 3:16, "All scripture is given by inspiration of God and is profitable for doctrine, for reproof, for correction, for instruction in righteousness."

The Bible can be used for the following:
- Teaching,

- Showing people their errors,
- Correction and
- Instruction in living a righteous life.

However, some teachers take the Bible out of context and mislead others. While I do not want you to worry, these are some of the signs that will arise before the time comes. I've just shared a number of things that we must look out for and be aware of before Jesus actually comes back.

Chapter 2 — The 2 Witnesses

Revelation 11:1-13 addresses the two witnesses, the last two major prophets on earth. Here is what the Scriptures say.

"Then I was given a reed like a measuring rod. And the angel stood, saying, 'Rise and measure the temple of God, the altar, and those who worship there. But leave out the court which is outside the temple, and do not measure it, for it has been given to the Gentiles. And they will tread the holy city underfoot for forty-two months. And I will give power to my two witnesses, and they will prophesy one thousand two hundred and sixty days, clothed in sackcloth. These are the two olive trees and the two lampstands standing before the God of the earth. And if anyone wants to harm them, fire proceeds from their mouth and devours their enemies. And if anyone wants to harm them, he must be killed in this manner. These have power to shut heaven, so that no rain falls in the days of their prophecy; and they have power over waters to turn them to blood, and to strike the earth with all plagues, as often as they desire. When they finish their testimony, the beast that ascends out of the bottomless pit will make war against them, overcome them, and kill them. And their dead bodies will lie in the street of the great city which spiritually is called Sodom and Egypt, where also our Lord was crucified. Then those from the peoples, tribes, tongues, and nations will see their dead bodies three-and-a-half days, and not allow their dead bodies to be put into graves. And those who dwell on the earth will rejoice over them, make merry, and send gifts to one another, because these two prophets tormented those who dwell on the earth.

Now after the three-and-a-half days the breath of life from God entered them, and they stood on their feet, and great fear fell on those who saw them. And they heard a loud voice from heaven saying to them, "Come up here." And they ascended to heaven in a cloud, and their enemies saw them. In the same hour there was a great earthquake, and a tenth of the city fell. In the earthquake seven thousand people were killed, and the rest were afraid and gave glory to the God of heaven."

Personal Story

First, I want to share a personal story.

Over 20 years ago, a person that I was seeing at the time told me that I was one of the prophets in Revelation 11. I always tend to pay more heed to people who tell me something about myself instead of drawing my own conclusions. At the time, it seemed like this person was on my side and had my best interests at heart.

However, after I thought about it and after other events came to light, she didn't have my best interests at heart and was trying to lead me into a breakdown by the way she treated me.

She asked me if I was a manic depressive, which is the old term for bipolar disorder. However, I didn't know what she was talking about. She then worked to keep me up for unreasonable hours and feed me controversial ideas and thoughts, which will send someone with a mental disorder over the edge.

She turned to Revelation 11, and she showed me the passage and told me that we were these two witnesses of this chapter. That sent me on a tail spin so that I started to have crazy thoughts. I had my first breakdown through a psychotic episode. I ended up in the hospital, telling doctors that I was one of these two prophets and that I had come to judge the world. Off and on, I think that I was under the delusion that I was one of the two witnesses for 16 years.

During that time, I went through all of the books of the prophets and looked at every Scripture and tried to discern the passages that were yet to be fulfilled and those that had come to pass.

I examined the book of Revelation multiple times. I was trying to work out what I needed to do so that I could both present the Gospel of Jesus Christ to the world and judge the world at the same time. I was trying to work out what sort of prophecies still needed to be fulfilled in the Old Testament and what scope I had as a person that would judge the world and what sort of judgements I could bring in. I had to work out how I could effectively judge the world and save the world at the same time.

You can imagine that 16 years of thinking that I was one of the two witnesses certainly took its toll on me. The lady who fed me these lies later denied that she was one of them and accused me of being crazy. We parted company.

Later on, I looked for another person who I basically talked into becoming the second prophet. We went on adventures and tried to fulfill some of the Scriptures by going to a town in Australia.

Some people out there in the world seem to think that they are one of the two witnesses because they believe satan and his demons.

This seems to be a clever way that satan takes hold of a Christian's life, someone who is passionate and zealous for the things of the Lord. Most often, satan speak through an antichrist spirit. This spirit masquerades as the Holy Spirit and fools a person by pretending to be Jesus' voice. The spirit will say things to the prophet and tell them that God has chosen them to be one of the two prophets.

A person might struggle to differentiate between the real Holy Spirit and an antichrist spirit. This deceiving spirit will cause you a lot of problems. This antichrist spirit will mislead you and tell you the wrong things.

For 16 years, I believed that I was one of the two witnesses. I did a lot of reading of Old Testament prophets and the book of Revelation. I searched out a lot of blog posts and internet sites about the two witnesses. I read many accounts of people talking about the two witnesses. I devoured all sorts of material, trying to search out information about the two witnesses and what they did, how they lived their lives and how they performed their ministry.

I found little information on what they actually do. However, I found some articles quoting Scripture, saying they'll strike the earth with many plagues as often as they wish. If people try to come against them, fire will come out of their mouth. People seemed to spend quite a bit of time trying to work out or explain who the two witnesses were. They wondered whether the two witnesses were Elijah and John, or Elijah and Moses, or Elijah and Enoch.

A lot of the posts, articles and information that I found on the two witnesses did not say what the two witnesses actually did. However, most of the information that I found discussed and tried to ascertain which two saints in the Bible were going to be used as the two witnesses on earth.

With that history, I stopped believing that I was one of the two witnesses about eight years ago. I've had time away from Revelation. For the last eight years, I have been in other parts of the Bible and finding some balance in my life.

I found that you can be too carried away with the book of Revelation with an intense fixation on it. Instead, you need to focus on loving God and loving your fellow man. After an extended season of focus of the Gospels and on Jesus, I have now been directed to write on Revelation through several prophetic words from God.

Who Are the 2 Witnesses?

Many thoughts and opinions are prevalent in the world about the identity of the two witnesses. I was listening to a popular preacher yesterday. Right in the middle of his sermon, he stated, "It's plain to see that Elijah and Moses are the two witnesses." He claims that they turn the waters into blood, which Moses did and fire comes out of their mouths, which Elijah did.

He insisted, "I don't know why people speculate or argue about that. It is really obvious."

When it comes to the book of Revelation, all you can really do is have an opinion. I find that Revelation seems to cause a lot of arguments, but here is my take on the identity of the two witnesses.

Hebrews 9:27 says, "And as it is appointed for men to die once, but after this the judgment."

According to that Scripture, people are to die once. The only two people that didn't die, according to the Bible, were Enoch and Elijah. Both of them were taken by God and went up to heaven.

I've read of an Indian apostle whose name is D.G.S. Dhinakaran. He has had visions of heaven and actually met Enoch and Elijah once in heaven. He tells this story in the book of visions that he had of heaven.[1]

Enoch and Elijah were there with Jesus, and they actually ask Jesus if it was their time to come to earth. Jesus answered, "No, you've got to wait awhile. It is not time." Jesus went on to tell this apostle from India that Enoch and Elijah were the two witnesses that were mentioned in Revelation that are due to come.

This Indian apostle has since died. However, when I read his book, his beliefs about Enoch and Elijah as the two witnesses made sense. He went on to quote the above verse in Hebrews 9.

---

[1] "Heavenly Visions of D.G.S. Dhinakaran (English)," Jesus Calls Publication, Chennai, 2008. P. 20.

Moses is likely not one of the two witnesses because it says in Jude that Michael and satan argued over Moses' body. Moses' body was buried by Michael when he died, so Moses is definitely dead.

We do not have multiple lives. Many Christians use this Scripture when people in the New Age mention that they've had past lives.

For the reasons listed, I personally believe that Elijah and Enoch are the two witnesses. Their exact identity doesn't really matter when it comes down to them actually appearing on earth. In any case, they will have power, authority and the ability to bring as many plagues as possible down on earth as often as they wish.

Revelation 11:6 tells us that they will walk in the miracles of Elijah — shutting heaven so that no rain falls — and in the miracles of Moses — striking the earth with all of the plagues that they desire.

They will come to earth with real power, causing droughts in countries that don't listen to what they say. They will be able to turn bodies of water into blood. They will be able to strike the earth with as many plagues as they want as often as they wish.

The two witnesses will be led by the Holy Spirit, following directions from God as the Holy Spirit inspires them to strike the earth with plagues. This doesn't mean that they are going to be out of control. Everything that they do will be intentional.

Will Arrive and Suddenly Do a Sign and a Wonder

The two witnesses will have power right away when they come. They are unlike people on earth who claim to be one of the two witnesses, who write blogs and books about prophecy or who try and release plagues and judgments on the earth through prophetic words and decrees. Unlike those people who are trying to build up a name for themselves and be recognized by the world, the two witnesses will arrive and do a sign and wonder on earth on their first day here.

They will immediately capture the world's attention. I will just paint a scenario for you as an example for you to consider. I am not saying that things will happen exactly this way, but this is similar to what they will do.

Imagine if the two witnesses came on television in the United States. Imagine if they stated, "We've got a list here of all of the names and the birthdates of every person in prison. We are like a modern-day Moses, and we are here to set the prisoners free. Isaiah 42 says that the servant of the Lord will set the prisoners free, which is what we are here to do. We don't agree with incarceration; we don't think that prison is the best place for rehabilitation. We have a database list of every prisoner who is incarcerated in America right now.

The second list is a list of prisoners that we want released. These people haven't committed violent crimes and will not do anything harmful in the future. However, these prisoners are confined on drug-related charges and for other minor offenses. We have set up places for these people to go. We've communicated with certain churches in the country that are ready to accept these prisoners and to rehabilitate them, so you need to let them go."

Imagine if that announcement was recorded for broadcast on American television. Imagine if the announcement also ordered, "You need to release these prisoners to these churches by a specific date and time, or the North Pacific Ocean will be turned to blood."

However, the American government will not respond to these unknown people even if the video goes viral on YouTube and even if the American people see this on the news.

At the appointed time, the North Pacific Ocean will turn to blood, and then the whole world will see that events happened just as the prophets warned. The whole world will see a replay of the threats and the instructions of the two witnesses on YouTube.

Then, the two witnesses will come back on television with a new date and time for the release of the prisoners. If the government does not comply, the Atlantic Ocean will turn to blood.

Once again, the American government will likely refuse to let the prisoners go despite the reality of the blood, the effect on marine life and the damage to the fishing industry. At the designated time, the Atlantic Ocean on the East coast will turn to blood.

Then, the two witnesses will come on TV again and state, "Now it is time for the American people to start a riot against their government because if the prisoners are not released by the appointed time, every single water source in America will turn to blood. All of your streams, lakes and all of your drinks and anything with water in it will turn to blood by the listed time. It is time to riot and tell your government that the prisoners are to be let go."

That final threat would easily cause the American population to riot, which would quickly escalate out of control.

That is just an example of something that might possibly happen with the two witnesses. While I do not know what they will do, I am just using this example to say that from the first day they arrive, they will perform a sign and a wonder. They will need to prove that they have the authority of God and will back this up with supernatural abilities.

It might be unfair of them to turn the oceans to blood before people can see that they are credible witnesses who have come from God. Even so, they could turn the oceans to blood very soon after they start their ministry.

The two witnesses aren't going to come to earth, hold conferences, write books and slowly build a platform to minister so that people will pay attention to them. Instead, they will come to earth and hit the ground running. According to Scripture, they will only be here for 1,260 days or three and a half years.

Amazingly enough, Jesus ministered on earth for three and a half years as well — about the same length of time as the two witnesses. The term of Jesus plus the term of the two witnesses is equal to seven years, the number of completion. God likes the number seven.

The two witnesses will be serious about their ministry. They are not going to come to earth and play with man. They will not just walk in a little anointing, similar to someone who ministers on earth, heals the sick and speaks at conventions.

The two witnesses will come with amazing power. Remember, if we look at the example of Moses, he totally destroyed an empire with 10 plagues.

The two witnesses will release some plagues. They will employ all manner of tactics to show an example to the world and to apply pressure on different facets, thoughts, industries, companies and countries in the world. They won't spend time trying to establish their platform.

Will Be Heavily into Justice and Righteousness

With the example of the incarcerated in prison and the ocean turning into blood, the two witnesses are basically echoing Moses, "Set my captives free; set my people free."

In Australia where I live, many of prisoners that are locked up are imprisoned on drug-related charges, such as taking or supplying drugs. They were convicted for selling drugs and trying to make enough money to buy their own drugs. These aren't necessarily the drug kingpins.

Some women go into prostitution while some men prostitute their women to raise money. Others don't have a girlfriend, so they turn to dealing drugs in order to pay for their habit.

Many men are in prison on drug-related charges. Prior to entering prison, about 10 percent of men and nearly 50 percent of women were sexually abused.[2] They might have turned to drugs to numb the pain of sexual abuse.

A focus on justice and someone who wants to make things right with victims, change the world and bring freedom and healing could do a lot with God's power. If you wanted to bring perpetrators of sexual abuse to justice, then the ability to bring plagues and perform other supernatural miracles could judge people.

Imagine if the two witnesses came to a country and stated, "From today on, drugs are illegal. Anyone who is addicted to heroin or ice or any other drug can now go to your tap and fill your bottle with water and say 'Bless me Jesus.' The water will sustain you with the feeling that the drug used to have. Over the next 30 days, the need for the drug will diminish, and you'll be clean and sober.

But from today onward, if you're selling drugs or supplying them to others, you will die of a heart attack."

---

[2]http://www.casaforchildren.org/site/c.mtJSJ7MPIsE/b.5525017/k.5115/Justice_Study_Prior_Abuse_Reported_by_Inmates.htm. Accessed September 24, 2016

Imagine if this stern warning went out on national TV to everyone who's supplying drugs in America. Imagine if they were warned that if they sell any more drugs, they're going to die of a heart attack. The Lord can cause a heart attack to come upon people. Perhaps only the people that see the warning would have the attacks, and the Lord would make sure that every supplier of drugs sees the warning before they die.

Imagine if anyone who has seen the warning from that time on saw all of the heart attacks start to happen as the video grows more popular. Imagine if everyone who's selling drugs dies of a heart attack.

Imagine if within one week of that announcement, no more drugs were sold in America.

You wouldn't need to spend billions of dollars building a wall in America to stop the Mexican influx of drugs. You wouldn't need the police force to try to capture people to stop the sale of drugs. You wouldn't have the corruption in governments and police forces when it comes to drugs. You wouldn't have drug cartels making billions of dollars supplying drugs. The population certainly wouldn't be strung out and wasting money on drugs.

Any drug addict who wanted the peace and joy of the Lord could simply pray over a bottle of water and say, "Bless me, Jesus."

The two witnesses would actually make water very popular by simply telling people who want to experience the peace and the joy of the Lord to fill a bottle with water and say, "Bless me Jesus." Then the person will feel the presence of God and the joy of the Lord.

This might have a two-fold effect that could stop people from taking drugs and turn them on to Jesus and his power, which satan wouldn't be able to copy and thus deceive people.

The two witnesses will have judgments like that. They will send plagues so that people respond.

According to the U.S. government, about 24.6 million or 9.4 percent of Americans over the age of 12 suffered from drug addiction in 2013.[3]

As of July 30, 2016, the Federal Bureau of Prisons reported that 46.4 percent — more than 84,000 people — were in custody for drug-related offenses.[4] The sheer numbers alone tell you how heavy this issue is on God's heart.

He is very burdened with the destruction and the loss of life due to the use of drugs.

Drug use will certainly be an issue with the two witnesses. He feels the same way about any issue related to justice.

If you don't believe that the two witnesses can cause a heart attack, they can certainly send a new angel of death.

The angel of death can revisit the world. The two witnesses might also say, "If you're a child sexual abuser, you need to report to your local police station and tell the police who you've been abusing. You need to call in the parents with evidence of who you have been abusing."

The police will send you to rehabilitation to help you recover. Many people don't believe that a pedophile can be rehabilitated, but as someone who has been bound in addiction for most of his life, I can tell you that freedom comes when the demons flee out of the person. When someone's demonically inspired and possessed, they can do drastic things. Once they are free of those demons and

---

[3] https://www.drugabuse.gov/publications/drugfacts/nationwide-trends. Accessed September 24, 2016.

[4] https://www.bop.gov/about/statistics/statistics_inmate_offenses.jsp. Accessed September 24, 2016.

free of the hurt and pain through deliverance and life counseling, change can happen.

Imagine if the two witnesses stated, "If you are a child sex offender, you have 24 hours to report to your local police station with evidence of the children you've offended and admission of your guilt. If you don't comply within 24 hours, you are going to die of a heart attack.

If you're a child or a parent who is watching this with a child who has been sexually abused, you need to report the offender to the police so that they can follow up on the case.

But most importantly, if you're a sex offender and you've been abusing children, you need to report to your local police station and confess your crimes, including every child that you've being abusing. Your life will be spared, and you can enter rehabilitation. But if you don't report to a police station within 24 hours, your life will be taken by God."

According to a report in the New York Times in 2011, nearly 20 percent of all women have been the victim of rape or an attempted rape.[5] A lot of men are perpetrators in these offenses. That doesn't even include the numbers of children who have been victimized.

You can imagine that these men don't want the embarrassment of public exposure of their crimes. They won't want to come forward and admit that they've been abusing others. It takes a lot of courage to come forward, and some of them would rather die than be embarrassed.

But with God, there's always grace. The people won't be imprisoned but will go into a rehabilitation program. The men will have a choice. While they won't like being in that position, the two

---

[5]http://www.nytimes.com/2011/12/15/health/nearly-1-in-5-women-in-us-survey-report-sexual-assault.html?_r=0. Accessed September 24, 2016.

witnesses will operate in justice. You can imagine all of the work for the two witnesses during the first month. First of all, they released the prisoners who were not a danger to society so that they could receive rehabilitation. Second of all, they stop all of the drug sales in the nation and set all of the drug addicts free with the peace and the presence of God filling them every day.

Then, they work on the real cause of drug addiction. They address the sexual abuse and the cause of the dysfunction. That means that every child in America who was currently being abused and crying out to God for their abuse to stop would see God answer their prayer.

A lot of families might lose a parent. A lot of fathers, stepfathers and scout leaders, as well as others who are involved in sexual abuse will disappear off the face of the earth. The ones who want to change and those who want help and those who want to live a life free of sexually abusing children will be delivered and set free.

I have been pondering these things for about 16 years since I believed that I was one of the two witnesses.

I believe the two witnesses will carry out these types of incidents — addressing every injustice in society and righting every wrong with a plague or a judgment. The abusers would be encouraged to repent and change their ways. Society would change very quickly.

Will Be Followed by the Media

We live in a world seemingly dominated by the media with graphic and horrific stories front and center.

When someone kills 50 people in a nightclub and goes on a shooting rampage, like what just happened in Orlando, the media is caught up in the death and with the scenes from the nightclub. Police will surround it. The media immediately goes to the scene, reporting the number of deaths and recording the carnage along with the graphic scenes.

Even if the two witnesses didn't have their own cameramen and their own team, everything that they said and did would still be captured by the media.

For example, as I'm preparing this book, Donald Trump is the Republican nominee for the President of the United States. Even though the media hates Donald Trump and is seriously against him, he receives a lot of coverage. After all, negative attention still means that he receives a lot of press.

The two witnesses will be front and center. The people of the world will quickly realize how serious the two witnesses are if they started their ministry by turning oceans into blood. You can imagine that the whole world will watch and listen to everything they have to say.

Even people that hate them will follow them. When they die, Revelation 11:10 says, "Those who dwell on the earth will rejoice over them, make merry, and send gifts to one another, because these two prophets tormented those who dwell on the earth."

When the two witnesses are killed and are left on the street not to be buried, the people of the world start a new Christmas and give each other gifts because the two prophets who've tormented the whole world are now dead.

Whoever hates the prophets will still watch the YouTube videos, media reports and everything that the two witnesses will be doing.

The two witnesses will be busy issuing threats, prophesying and commanding events to happen. They will not sit on their laurels while they're waiting, just passing the time.

Instead, they'll have a camera crew that will capture everything that they say and upload it to YouTube or social media. The people of the world will watch and follow everything that they say and do.

The two witnesses will be scary even more so than the antichrist. I envision that many people of the world will not like them, but the two witnesses will achieve everything that they want to achieve.

Will Translocate from One Country to Another

For example, when the ocean turns into blood, the two witnesses might be in San Francisco. They might say, "We warned you that this would happen."

From that moment on, the snipers and the CIA and the people that hire professional killers for government will be after the two witnesses to shoot them.

The two witnesses won't walk around that city in public when professional hit men are on their way. Instead, they will disappear from there and show up somewhere else.

They'll appear with their camera crew in another country and issue another command and judgment. Once they finish there, they will move to another country. They won't have passports. Countries won't necessarily want them to visit. They will officially be listed by the world government as terrorists. They won't be able to get a visa to travel on airplanes in ordinary ways.

They will translocate just as Philip in the Bible did after he preached to the Ethiopian eunuch when he traveled in the spirit to another place. The two witnesses will journey from country to country with their support team and the media. They will pronounce judgments and release God's justice and righteousness to the world.

They won't go to the visa office or to the consulate and request visas to travel between countries. They will just travel from country to country and do the Lord's pleasure and bidding wherever they go.

Bring Every Nation to Account before God

Some popular teachers have spoken about the two witnesses. They seem to believe that the two witnesses will stay in Jerusalem, declaring judgments without leaving the city. These same people also believe that Michael is the angel of Israel who doesn't travel anywhere else.

I find this to be a little narrow minded. The two witnesses are sent to earth to bring judgments to the earth along with God's justice and righteousness. It makes little sense to believe that they would only appear in Jerusalem. We know that the best way to address the American people or even the President of the U.S. isn't to say something in Jerusalem but to be present in the U.S. so that Americans can watch the broadcast on live TV.

The two witnesses will travel from nation to nation all across the world and spend their time going to different countries to bring each one into account with God. Some nations will come into alignment with the two witnesses. The two witnesses will actually meet with the leaders of the country and negotiate with them.

Some countries will follow God and be happy to do what the two witnesses say. I feel that some African nations and some Asian countries, perhaps even Australia, will invite the two witnesses to their countries.
They'll be willing to negotiate with the two witnesses and obey the Lord. Those nations will become followers of Jesus and dedicate their country and their population to Jesus. They will come into line with what the Kingdom of God wants and come out of alignment with the one-world government and what they want to happen.

The two witnesses will translocate and travel to each nation so that they can address the kings and the leaders of those nations and bring justice and righteousness to each country.

They'll be powerful. Many times, God has moved and done things in the history of the earth. He's used one or two people because he doesn't need millions of people to do his will.

When he gives two individuals his power to do whatever they choose to do, such as strike the earth with as many plagues as often as they wish, this will affect the world. When that power is given to two people, he can do marvelous and amazing things.

You can be sure that the two witnesses have evidence of every wrong thing that's been done in each country, including the behavior of corrupt politicians and the names and birthdates of every other unethical person in the country.

The two witnesses will be able to call out people and bring them to justice. Heaven has databases and records of everyone on earth and what each person does.

They'll have supernatural intelligence that far surpasses that of the CIA. Their intelligence comes directly from God. They have the truth, not a contrived lie or an angle that benefits a certain government or a certain position. They'll have the real truth about every individual, every country and every country's officials.

Bring Individual Companies to Account before God

Another major influence that the two witnesses will have is with individual companies.

The two witnesses will know which companies are operating unjustly in the world. They'll be aware of the businesses that are trading in certain ways and behaving in harmful ways toward others. Certain companies use cheap labor and even slave labor without paying for it.

The two witnesses will be aware of the practices of every business across the globe. The Lord might just send them individual reports on their computer so that they can address the infractions of these companies and bring them into line to God's way of doing things.

God will be aware of which boards of those businesses will respond to correction from the Lord. He will know which companies won't respond favorably to the two witnesses.

God will perform a reshifting and realignment in businesses. He will put some companies with unjust practices out of business. However, he will promote the businesses that are righteous and that are operating properly.

The two witnesses will not only affect governments and major areas of concern, such as drugs, crime, prisoners and matters related to God's righteousness and judgments, but will also impact individual companies, taking action and decreeing judgments.

While they are waiting for the government to decide if they will obey the order to release the prisoners before the oceans turn to blood, they might travel around America for those few days and decree judgments on certain companies while working with other businesses. If the oceans turn to blood, the whole world will be seriously affected.

God can release judgments and do anything that he chooses to do. These two men, imbued with the power of God, can really do anything.

The 10 plagues of Moses actually decimated Egypt through 10 days of visitations and judgment. Although I don't know how long it took for Moses' 10 judgments to happen, the judgments of the two witnesses will occur over 1,260 days. The two witnesses will have power to do what they want for quite a long time. They will bring individual companies into an account with God.

Will Reign at the Same Time as Antichrist

I personally believe that the two witnesses will be alive and giving their prophecies and releasing their judgments at the same time as the antichrist. I personally don't believe that the antichrist will rule at a separate time from the two witnesses. I believe that the two witnesses will have no fear of the antichrist, and they'll certainly be messing up his agenda.

I feel that secretly, a groundswell of Christians and even non-believers will really enjoy everything that the two witnesses do. They will really happy to tune in and watch what they do along with the reactions of the world.

I don't believe that the antichrist and the two witnesses will be on earth at two separate times. I will not say much about the antichrist at this point in the book. However, I just want you to know that I personally believe that the two witnesses will be real heroes to follow on earth, and it will be an exciting time as Christians watch the effect of the two witnesses and the radical judgments that they release.

Will Teach the Whole World to Fear and Revere God

The two witnesses will bring a new respect for God. People will realize that they speak with real power and authority. They will say something and then what they say will happen.

For example, they might say that any person dealing drugs from now on will die. When millions of people die who are all drug dealers, the people of the world will find a new respect for God. People who don't believe in God will suddenly be confronted with his reality.

The Scripture that says the knowledge and the glory of the Lord will be known throughout the whole world. Habakkuk 2:14 will definitely be fulfilled by the two witnesses. They will show the enormity and the massive power that's behind God and his two prophets.

The world will come to realize that these two prophets serve a real God who is interested in justice and righteousness. This God believes in love, compassion and grace and wants people set free and restored to the original person that they were meant to be.

The two witnesses will bring a newfound respect for God. People will begin to revere him, and Christians will come to a new realization of who God is.

People who aren't Christians will come to fear both this God of the two witnesses and fear the two witnesses. They won't have any way to argue against the two witnesses, no matter what their opinion of the two witnesses is. They'll come to realize that the two witnesses walk in power and authority.

The media might report that the two witnesses will be here for 1,260 days with rumors that the two witnesses won't be around forever.

They will admit that they have only a limited time on earth, but this won't affect the power and the authority and the potency of the two witnesses.

God and the two witnesses that he has sent will command the respect of the people who are living in the world at that time. The two witnesses will really prove that God is supernatural and powerful, and you can't argue with him. If you try to argue with the two witnesses, you will come out on the wrong side of the argument.

Finally, the atheists of the world who cry out for proof that there is a God will be shown proof of him. No one will be able to watch the accounts or videos of the two witnesses and see what they threaten and hear what they say will happen and then see those events come to pass without being affected. No one will be able to watch and still be able to say that there is no God. Of course, people will arise and say that the two witnesses are nothing more than two great magicians, yet no one will be able to duplicate the wonders that the two witnesses perform.

Will Inspire and Interact with 144,000

I'm going to discuss the 144,000 later in the book, but for now, I personally feel that the 144,000 is just a figure of 12 times 12 times 10 times 10 times 10. I feel that this is a significant figure to God. I also think that the New Jerusalem that comes down from heaven will be 144,000 cubits.

I feel that this figure represents something important to God, and the 144,000 will possibly be millions of people who are dedicated to him and who want to serve the Lord in a fuller capacity than the average Christian — people who obey the Lord in everything he says and does and people who are set apart for him.

These are people who focus their whole lives on God and on his Kingdom. I feel that God will use many people to do miracles in the last days. The two witnesses will inspire and interact with those people.

I believe that the two witnesses will have social media accounts and ways to contact these on-fire Christians. They will have staff to work with them, a staff of people who are satisfied by God with an income to be financed by God. I feel that the two witnesses will have a strong staff with a great support team. I feel that certain people who love God will be able to get in touch with the two witnesses to talk and interact with them.

I think that many of the millions of people that are represented by the 144,000 will be able to meet and interact with the two witnesses. These individuals will listen to everything that the two witnesses say and do.

These people will co-labor with the two witnesses and continue with a similar anointing. They will perform signs and wonders and take action against companies. They might use the information that the two witnesses have brought down from heaven.

Some of these people will be connected with the two witnesses and will even receive assignments from the two witnesses where they will be given authority and permission to accomplish certain things on the earth. I feel that these people will have a similar ministry as the two witnesses with power allotted to them by God. They will not only be inspired by and interact with the two witnesses but will also co-labor with them and perform similar feats both where they live and where they travel.

I also believe that these people will be able to translocate and travel supernaturally. Many of them won't have visas or passports because they will be targeted as renowned cross followers who are dangerous to the population of the earth and dangerous in the eyes of the world government and their view of good and evil.

The two witnesses will be heroes to the 144,000. They will co-labor together, increasing their effectiveness.

Information from heaven will be supplied to the 144,000, such as the databases on the corrupt companies and the crooked politicians. The 144,000 will then enact judgments against the countries.

Will Speak on Behalf of God and Make His Demands Known

The two witnesses won't speak on their own but will be fully led by the Holy Spirit. Of course, they will deal with emotions and appetites and be affected by the human condition like anyone is. They will participate in normal, daily activities, such as dressing, sleeping, meditation, prayer, and going out to dinner with people and interacting with them. Yet when they speak, they'll speak on behalf of God, and they'll bring his demands and his messages to the world.

The whole world will know who they are. People who hate them will still listen to what they have to say. For example, many people who hate Trump still listen to some of the things he says, which makes them even angrier at his words.

Many people who don't like the message or the authority of the two witnesses will still listen to what they say. They will be addicted to watching what the two witnesses do as they bring messages to the world directly from God and the throne room.

Never in the history of mankind will anyone have such a huge audience as the two witnesses. The people who listen to them won't be converted believers, but you can be sure that the two witnesses will share the Gospel and the salvation message.

They will not be on earth just to announce doom and gloom. Each of the judgments will have a grace component so that each person who is about to be judged will have an alternative so that he or she can make a righteous decision — a decision for Christ. If they don't make a righteous decision, then they will be judged. God is still a God of mercy.

Certain companies are acting wickedly. The Lord knows that if they are threatened in the right way, they will change their ways. For others, no amount of coercion will change their minds. God will take down these companies and destroy them through the judgments.

The two witnesses will have an audience with the world. As such, those who listen will be people that are set apart with a mission.

You can understand that if Enoch and Elijah came from many thousands of years ago, they won't waste their time here. They haven't spent thousands of years in heaven, waiting to be released to the earth for them to just waste time.

They're not coming to earth to make friends and to make disciples. They're not coming to the world to be loved and appreciated.

Instead, they will come to earth with a mission. They will be sent by God just like Moses was sent to release the Israelites from Egypt. He was sent to achieve a special mission for God.

The two witnesses will be sent to the world with a message and a reason. From day one to day 1,260, they're going be on point — on a mission as they say and do everything that God has required of them.

They will have free will, and I've read into the passage that they'll strike the earth with as many plagues as often as they wish. The words, "as often as they wish," are in that Scripture, which means that they may withhold plagues, or they may increase plagues, depending on how they feel and on the response of the people.

Certain companies and even some countries might not respond the way that they envisioned. They might have to perform an extra plague to bring the country into line. They will have authority, but they will also have free will. They will be individuals with their own personalities. God will use them mightily; people will listen to their message.

Many people will be scared into the Kingdom. For example, when people watch a movie with a vigilante who takes justice into his own hands, they cheer on the vigilante in the movie because they want to see justice done.

Just like a vigilante in a film, the same will be true of the two witnesses. Many people who were formerly skeptics and who couldn't ordinarily be convinced of God's righteousness will see:

- the two witnesses deal with the drug problem on the earth
- the prisoners be released and rehabilitated
- wicked corporations tumble and
- governments fall.

They will see the effect that the two witnesses are having, and they'll become converted. They'll come around to the way of thinking that the two witnesses are proposing. They'll realize that God really is a God of justice and that he really does care about people and that he does take action.

Many people who were previously skeptics and who felt that God doesn't care about justice and righteousness and that he won't do anything about these situations will be convinced and will become powerful supporters of the two witnesses.

The two witnesses won't lack for finances, media attention or any good thing. They will be supplied by God and resourced and empowered by him. They're going to deliver God's messages.

Will Prove that God Exists and Show His Power Through what They Do

So far, we have covered that the two witnesses will show that God exists. People will no longer be in no man's land, wondering about the reality of God. He will have two representatives on earth to prove the existence of Christ.

The two witnesses will have power over the elements. If a country does not conform to what they say, they will send plagues to it, such as stopping the rain, and they will totally bring the nation to its knees. The two witnesses will have amazing and extraordinary power. They could even cause rainfall over the farm estates of the righteous people in the country while no rain falls on the rest of the country.

The two witnesses can do anything to convince the people of the world that there is a God. Just to repeat the verse that I mentioned before, the knowledge of the glory of the Lord will be known throughout the whole world as the waters cover the sea.

The glory of the Lord will be seen through the two witnesses and through the figurative number of 144,000 disciples as mentioned in the book of Revelation.

They will prove that God exists. Of course, the obstinate and stubborn people of the world will say that the actions of the two witnesses can be explained by magic. Certain people on earth will refuse to admit that God is acting through the two witnesses.

Many religious people will rise up and even accuse the two witnesses of being the antichrist or the false prophet. They might try to spread that rumor.

At the same time, they might even elect the antichrist and false prophet to a political position as an answer to the two witnesses. I'm not sure how that will play out, but I'm sure that many people will come to God during this time. They'll believe that God exists and come to respect and revere the power that is coming through the two witnesses.

Will Share the Gospel with the World

The two witnesses will share the message of salvation and that Jesus loves the people of the world. Their plagues will be strategic plagues.

They will plan strategic strikes just like when America strikes the enemy and takes down their communication, ammunition bases and weapons' storages. The attacks and the airplane raids by the United States against a country are not indiscriminate but strategic.

The two witnesses will plan intentional plagues with a purpose and a reason. They won't set up plagues just for the sake of hurting people.

People will realize that God planned for the two witnesses to stage these surgical strikes. They're cutting out evil just like a surgeon who cuts out the cancer in a person.

The two witnesses will come to the world and surgically remove the cancer and the disease — cutting out much of the evil in the world.

When they're preaching that Jesus loves you and wants to save you, the message might not make sense to some people because it seems that the two witnesses are killing all sorts of evil people.

People who have a heart for justice and who have common sense will realize that the two witnesses are really acting on God's behalf and doing what he would do if he were on earth. They will implement surgical strikes against the evil in the world.

These will be well planned, organized and orchestrated. The two witnesses will seem to have intelligence that surpasses that of the world. They'll have information on their computer databases about everyone that they're targeting.

When the two witnesses preach the Gospel of salvation as well as the 144,000 that are represented in the Bible, a movement of people will turn from the darkness of the world to the light of Christ.

Many people teach that Jesus will come before the tribulation and that Christians won't suffer through the tribulation. I feel that it will be very unfair for the people of the world to miss out on going to heaven without really being shown the answer of a God who is powerful and resourceful and who cares about justice. The world needs to see God take a stand against injustice.

I feel that as the 144,000 people go out and preach the Gospel and as the two witnesses judge the world in righteousness, then the world will come to realize that God is real and cares for them.

Everyone that the two witnesses and the 144,000 can save will be saved. God will use the two witnesses and the 144,000 to impact his world, and when they're finished, he'll be finished.

Will Use Every Day of the 1,260 Days to Maximum Effect

Like I've shared before, the two witnesses won't waste time. Of course, they'll spend two hours or as long as necessary meeting with key individuals or with a country's leaders.

Even so, they won't waste time on activities like watching TV, going to movies or going out for coffee. Whenever they eat, go out for coffee and even when they're alone, they'll be doing something productive.

Every time they go out to eat or even just for coffee, they'll schedule an important meeting. The two witnesses will have plenty to say to each other and will bounce all of their ideas off each other as they explain their thoughts. They'll have an inner circle of people, people of influence that will be powerfully used by the Lord. The inner circle will perform a lot of exploits, according to the instructions of the two witnesses, with the same anointing and power.

Their inner circle will surround them when they go out for meals and will be part of their staff that helps them administrate and manage their ministry. They will be important to the two witnesses and serve their ministry.

However, the two witnesses will not waste even one of the 1,260 days that they spend on earth. They will hit the ground running and do everything that they have been commanded to do.

They will shock the world. The whole world will know who they are and will be in awe of them. Everyone will hear their message; whether or not they respond to that message is another subject, but everyone will know that God is not happy.

Everyone will hear that God won't tolerate injustice forever and that salvation comes through Jesus Christ. Everyone will see what the two witnesses do when they're on earth. They won't waste time.

They might speak at conferences in stadiums and instruct the people, but I feel that most of their speaking will be done over the internet. They will use social media and TV broadcasts as a platform. I can see satellite TVs and Christian television scheduling a lot of time for the two witnesses. I can see them having strategic alliances with global Christian television programs. I can sense that God will reach a lot of people who ordinarily wouldn't be saved through the message of the two witnesses.

Will Encourage Christians to Be Hot for Jesus and not Lukewarm

A well-known Scripture in Revelation 3:15-17 tells us: "I know your works, that you are neither hot nor cold. I could wish you were cold or hot. So then, because you are lukewarm, and neither cold nor hot, I will vomit you out of my mouth because you say 'I and rich, have become wealthy, and have need of nothing'—and do not know that you are wretched, miserable, poor, blind and naked."

I feel that before Jesus vomits certain Christians out of his mouth, the lukewarm Christians will need to make a decision while the two witnesses are here. They can become obstinate and rebel against God and his ways, or they can be hot and on fire for God.

There won't be any middle ground when the two witnesses are here. People will see the God of Abraham, the God of Elijah and

Moses. They'll see him in action, which will blast people out of complacency.

For too long, the church has been preaching that all you've got to do is accept Jesus and then you can still be a friend of the world and continue to have all the best the world can offer. You can have Jesus as a side benefit in your life. You might feel that you can treat Jesus like an accessory in your life, like a handbag for a woman that she chooses to match her outfit instead of the most important thing in the world that you need.

The two witnesses will blast people out of complacency and set certain people's hearts on fire for God. They will realize that God means business and that he is against injustice and full of mercy and is a God who judges between the righteous and the unjust. He is a God that greatly cares about people.

Malachi 3:16-18 states, "Then those who feared the Lord spoke to one another, And the Lord listened and heard them; So a book of remembrance was written before Him For those who fear the Lord And who meditate on His name. 'They shall be Mine,' says the Lord of hosts, 'On the day that I make them My jewels. And I will spare them As a man spares his own son who serves him.' Then you shall again discern Between the righteous and the wicked, Between one who serves God And one who does not serve Him."

The two witnesses will make a clear line of demarcation between the wicked and the righteous. They will allow people to discern the difference for themselves.

The Lord says to Malachi that he will spare the people that fear him like a father spares his own son. The Lord will allow judgments to reign down from the two witnesses, yet the righteous will be spared from those judgments. Ten thousand might fall at one side, and 10,000 might fall on the other side, but the righteous will be spared.

Christians will be encouraged and fired up and motivated to become hot Christians. They're not going to be lukewarm anymore.

Every Sign and Wonder Will Be Used to Maximum Effect

The two witnesses won't put a half-hearted effort into signs and wonders. Each one that they do will be used for the maximum effect.

They will use the plagues and the signs and wonders that they do to liberate, change, transform, judge and redeem the world. The two witnesses won't waste their breath, words, prophecies or judgments. Everything they do will be used for the greatest possible impact.

Even the first signs and wonders that the two witnesses perform, such as turning the water into blood on both coasts of America, will be used for the maximum effect of putting the whole world in fear. Then, the whole world will recognize and revere the two witnesses. Even people that don't like them will respect them.

They will build on signs, wonders and miracles — one after another. When they perform signs and wonders here in America, the whole world will pay attention.

However, places without access to the news, such as India or parts of Asia or villages in Africa, might have not heard of that sign or wonder. The two witnesses will go to Africa and Asia and do works there to gain the attention of those people. They will go to every country and work in each location to impact that nation.

The two witnesses won't be trying to build up themselves or their own personal brand. They won't hold back on what they say for fear of political correctness. They won't hold back on the judgments they make. They will do everything that God commands them to do and act as they're led by the Holy Spirit.

They won't walk in fear of men, the antichrist, false prophets, demons or satan. They won't fear anyone.

After they finish their day's work and go to sleep wherever they are, they will get up in the morning and do another full 12 hours work for the Kingdom of God.

They won't take days off or even tire out. They won't waste any of the signs or wonders that they do. They will focus on making a maximum impact with everything that they do.

Will Meet Leaders of Countries

Certain countries will be open to the two witnesses and will welcome what they do.

Some countries might take a while to warm up to them, but they will send a message to the two witnesses' administration to set up a meeting with them so that they can align their country with the two witnesses. The country will come into alignment with God and his purposes.

The two witnesses will meet with the leaders of the nations to organize meetings. The country will become righteous in God's sight, and God will work with the nation so that good things happen with them going forward.

Of course, the two witnesses might recommend a lot of changes for the nation, according to what God wants. The leaders of the country will implement those changes.

Will Have Snipers Trying to Shoot Them

After the two witnesses have increased in popularity, the world government and other global leaders will call professional hit men to shoot the two witnesses.

Many times, the snipers will have the two witnesses in their sights and will take aim. However, the bullets will be misdirected as they approach the two witnesses, missing them or disappearing completely, depending on what the angel or what God wants to do with the bullet.

Snipers will shoot at the two witnesses for years and years. However, on the final day, I personally believe that the two witnesses will be continuing with business as usual. This time, the snipers will line up the shot and shoot them, hitting and killing them.

I don't believe that the two witnesses will be captured or tortured in any way but believe that they will face a quick death. Revelation states that the two witnesses will lie on the ground for three and a half days.

Revelation 11:11, 12 tells us, "Now after three-and-a-half days the breath of life entered them, and they stood on their feet, and great fear fell on those who saw them. And they heard a loud voice from heaven saying to them, 'Come up here.' And they ascended to heaven in a cloud, and their enemies saw them."

The two witnesses will be killed and stay dead and unburied for three days. Once they are dead, people will exchange gifts and have a party. The two witnesses will ascend to heaven. When the two witnesses go up in the cloud, when they rise from the dead, **I personally believe that the rapture will happen at that time.**

I believe when the two witnesses and the 144,000 have finished their testimony, the world will have finally been warned and finally been shown the answer.

I believe that as the two witnesses ascend into the clouds, then Jesus will send the angels out and collect everyone who's still alive — those who are Christians who have been saved by the two witnesses and the 144,000.

I believe that all of these individuals will go to heaven at that moment. I don't believe they'll go to heaven beforehand unless they die as a martyr in the tribulation.

If you like, you can feel free to disagree with me, but that's what I personally believe.

Revelation 11:5 states, "And if anyone wants to harm them, fire proceeds from their mouth and devours their enemies. And if anyone wants to harm them, he must be killed in that manner."

I've had a lot of revelations about the two witnesses as you can see from what I've written here. However, I haven't had any revelation about the fire coming out of their mouth, devouring people. I know Elijah sent fire on a company of 50 men on two separate occasions. This got the king's attention and the attention of the next commander, and Elijah didn't kill the commander when he came for him.

I don't have any revelation on fire coming out of the mouths of the two witnesses and killing their enemies. If fire actually destroyed anyone that came after the two witnesses, this would be a potent act indeed.

I believe that the angels could kill anyone who tries to kill the two witnesses, including any snipers that take a shot at them. Word might get out that if you're going to be a sniper who attempts to kill the two witnesses, then you'd better kill them, or you will die.

I'm not sure how that will happen. I feel that if I were meant to have revelation on that, then the Lord would have given me a revelation over the years on it. However, since I've never received any revelation on it, I don't feel it's that important, but I certainly wouldn't try and kill the two witnesses.

That's my teaching on the two witnesses. I hope it's been informative. Once again, I want to share with you that I'm only a person, and I'm not infallible. This teaching can be taken with a grain of salt and simply viewed as a guide on what I believe the two witnesses will be up to and how they will operate. You can also dismiss this teaching.

Chapter 3 — The End Time Church

What I'm going to share with you next is a number of visions that I've had about the future and what I believe will happen to the church.

Of course, I'm not infallible, and I could be wrong. That remains to be seen. However, this is what I see in the future. I have shared this vision with other people before. A couple of people have told me that they have heard other notable preachers share the same thing. I hope that I'm right and that those notable preachers are right. I pray that you'll be blessed by reading this chapter.

First of all, for a long time, I was impressed with the church at Philadelphia mentioned in Revelation. I think that the Lord pointed out that church to me many years ago so that I would ponder over the church.

Revelation 3:7-10 states the following:

> "And to the angel of the church in Philadelphia write, 'These things says He who is holy, He who is true, "He who has the key of David, He who opens and no one shuts, and shuts and no one opens" "I know your works. See, I have set before you an open door, and no one can shut it; for you have a little strength, have kept My word, and have not denied My name. Indeed I will make those of the synagogue of Satan, who say they are Jews and are not, but lie—indeed I will make them come and worship before your feet, and to know that I have loved you. Because you have kept My command to persevere, I also will keep you from the hour of trial which shall come upon the whole world, to test those who dwell on the earth."

Many people look at that Scripture and believe that they're going to escape the judgments that are coming to the whole world because they are righteous and they persevered. They believe that they are going to be raptured out of the last days and not go through them.

However, Moses went through the judgments. He was on earth when the nation of Egypt was judged and was with the Israelites in Egypt when it was judged. They went through the trial.

Noah was on earth during an act of judgment. He went through the trial that came upon the whole earth. Lot was on earth when Sodom was judged.

You don't necessarily have to be in heaven to escape the trial that comes upon the earth. You just would need to be in another place — another geographical location when the judgment hits.

The Israelites painted their doors with the blood of their lambs and when the angel of death came, he killed all the first-born children of the houses that didn't have the blood of the lamb on the door post.

In a similar fashion, God can use judgments although they might not affect believers. The Lord will allow certain people to die, and he will be righteous in his judgments.

First of all, Jesus doesn't say anything bad about this church. This church actually existed in Turkey at the time of John's writing. While the letter was for the church at that time, it is also a prophetic word speaking of today's time.

Jesus does not have any negative words for another church in Revelation called Smyrna. The people in that church will be in a trial that will last ten days.

Jesus really loves these Philadelphian pastors. Like I said, I've had my eye on this church for a number of years. I feel that they are a special group of Christians with a caring pastor that Jesus really loves.

The people in the church of Philadelphia are the people who love Jesus with all their heart, and they are focused on Jesus with their whole lives revolving around him.

They would do anything for Jesus, and their whole lives are filled with his desires and with his presence. Ordinarily, they always do what they feel that Jesus wants them to do.

If they found a book on the 50 commands of Jesus, and they realized that Jesus wanted them to obey these commands, they'd get out the commands and then start to follow them.

If they knew of a book on how to be set apart for God and how to be holy and how to not live for the world, they would do what that book said.

They would do anything to be effective in their Christian walk and to draw closer to Jesus and to love others more. If they saw a person with a more intimate relationship with Jesus, they would strive to be like that person. They would do whatever they could do to become a better Christian and walk more closely with Jesus.

These people aren't always the richest or those with the most education. Remember, Revelation says, "For you have little strength: But have kept my word and not denied my name." These passionate people for Jesus are found in every church at the moment; every denomination has a group of them.

Some people teach that only 5 to 10 percent of Christians will be taken in the rapture. While I don't believe that, I have to say that the Lord considers a large percentage of Christians lukewarm.

A saying has gone around Christian circles. "If Christianity was a crime, would they find enough evidence to convict you?"

The Philadelphian Christian is one whose whole life is set apart and whose whole life is devoted to Jesus and to doing his will on earth. They want to co-labor with Jesus and participate in bringing his Kingdom to earth.

The Lord will start with a lot of Philadelphian pastors. The church often receives its vision and direction through the pastor of the church. They might have a board of elders, but the pastor almost always sets the course of the church. Jesus will choose certain pastors with the Philadelphian mindset. According to this passage, he will cause revival to break out in these congregations of Philadelphian pastors.

He will move on the five-fold ministry in these churches. All of the five-fold ministers — the apostles, prophets, evangelists, pastors and the teachers — in these churches will be set on flame by Jesus to do great things. The evangelist might preach at the church, holding revival meetings, and the church will take off and gain a reputation for signs and wonders.

Similar to Bethel Church in Redding, California, led by Bill Johnson, these churches will enter a season of revival where people come to the Lord in large numbers. Others will be healed, and signs and wonders will be done in the church.

The churches will have a name for themselves. They will have a reputation in the Christian church. People quickly hear when revival hits a church.

God will move through prayer, through a holy and devoted people and through his Spirit in many churches all at once. He won't necessarily need an evangelist or a preacher to come to the church to start a revival. The Lord will answer the prayers of the pastors' hearts who are seeking for more of God and who are looking for him to move. He will start to move and bring these churches into revival.

Christians who are part of this church will have business ideas. They will receive downloads from heaven about business concepts and inventions. These Philadelphian Christians will be aligned with churches that are going into revival. People will ask for support from the church to start their inventions and products and to launch their businesses.

The churches will have the same Holy Spirit speak to them that moved in the early church. The Holy Spirit will speak to them and lead them, just like in the book of Acts. Acts 2:44, 45 tells us, "Now all who believe were together and had all things in common, and sold their possessions and goods, and divided them among all as anyone had need."

The same Holy Spirit that moved upon the early church in Acts will move these people into an understanding that everything that we possess is ours, and everything that we possess is common to all. The Holy Spirit will start to move some of these churches to form communities, sell property and move from certain locations to other locations. They will buy property in the same suburb, move in together and start to form something similar to gated communities, where they will live and congregate together.

This might happen quickly as persecution starts to come to the church with the rise of political correctness and of Islam in Western nations. This might put pressure on Christians, and they might decide to sell property in multiple suburbs of the city, moving to one location and forming communities there.

Whatever event motivates this to happen, I sense a return to the book of Acts as Christians will pool their resources, share their money and give to those who are out of work. In their communities, they will support people who need money.

Now, people sometimes start cults with similar ideas in mind. The leader asks the people to sell what they have and move to a community that he chooses where he will lead them. When they start forming a community under someone, the Christian church far and wide will label this community of faith a cult. However, I am not referring to these groups as cults as they will not walk in error.

When Christians start to bond together and have all things in common and share as a community, the religious church don't seem to like it. However, these pastors and churches will be in revival as the inventions start to take off and the money starts to come in, which is the spirit of the early church.

An invention by one person in the congregation will be considered an invention by all. The money and the finances of the new businesses, inventions and products will go towards the church community. The church will work together as people in the church community offer their services to others. More inventions and products will be created. People that move into the community will find work in those organizations, and the Christian community will start to grow.

God will pour out his favor and blessing on the businesses. These businesses will be favored by the Lord and have doors opened to them.

Revelation 3:7 tells us, "…He who is holy, He who is true, 'He who is the king of David, He who opens and no one shuts, and shuts and no one opens.' "

The Lord will open doors for these businesses and give them favor. No one will shut the doors on these companies because God himself will open the doors.

As the church community grows, they will come under persecution, and the religious, traditional church will call them a cult.

Verse 9 of the same chapter says, "Indeed, I will make those of the synagogue of Satan, who say they're Jews and are not, but lie—

indeed I will make them come and worship before your feet, and to know that I've loved you."

Opposition will come. The religious church will rise up and call these churches cults. The revival churches will link up across denominations, across all racial barriers and across countries.

The churches that move in revival will connect through the internet and through open doors to each other. The pastors of different denominations will leave their denomination or will become part of this new church, this new movement that is going to sweep the world.

People in five-fold ministry and those who are part of the 144,000 will meet and cross pollinate with each other. People from one church in revival will travel to another church in revival where they will preach. Through these connections, the communities will grow in each country and across America.

The churches' communities will grow and become larger and larger. More Christians will start moving in to the church community and sharing their possessions. They will live together, and their children will attend school in the same place. They will buy their products from the same stores and live in community together.

Preachers and ministers and others with these giftings will arise out of these revival churches and will become guest speakers in other churches that aren't yet having revival. When they are invited to speak at these churches, they'll move in signs and wonders and start to light fires of revival there.

The minister of these churches will be a Philadelphian pastor who wants revival. He'll be open to inviting a pastor from a church that is already in revival. Shifts will start to happen. Many of the people in the churches that are in revival will travel to other churches that are not part of the program or part of the group of revival churches yet. They will preach in other churches that will come into revival and join with the revival churches.

The revival churches will grow and grow. They will eventually book stadiums for outreaches. They will create more products. Others will have product ideas at these revival churches. Then, the products and brands will emerge from them. They will have the Lord's favor and will see great success.

The church will become global and will start to move away from the other churches. They will link up with each other through a portal on the internet. They will likely start to work together as one church body across many states and countries.

They might call themselves, "The Bride of Christ," "The Elect," "The Church of Philadelphia" or a similar name.

The revival churches will move away from traditional churches and start to associate with other churches in revival. They will send out evangelists, preachers, apostles, teachers and prophets to other churches to bring them into the flock and into revival.

As other churches come into revival, the Christians in these churches will start to form communities as they did in the book of Acts when they shared all things, had everything in common and built communities of their own.

The church will also be known by their products and the brands that they release. These brands will become more and more popular in the marketplace.

More and more of these churches will arise, and more and more of these communities will form. More and more Christians will start to flock to these communities and churches.

Whenever pastors invite the revival ministers from those churches to preach in their church, that church will suddenly come into revival.

This will be similar to the Toronto blessing. When the Toronto blessing broke out in the '90s, everyone who traveled to Toronto got a taste of the Toronto blessing and brought it back to their church. Then, their church, no matter where in the world it was located, broke out with the same blessing from Toronto.

Similarly, these churches will grow and start to explode and will win thousands upon thousands of people to the Lord. As signs and wonders break out and as the churches exponentially increase, people from these churches will form the 144,000. Each of them will be compelled to preach, and they will be motivated to spend their whole life serving God.

Some of the 144,000 will go to other churches and preach and spark revival there. These new churches will come into alignment with the body of churches that are already in revival. The new church will rise up and become a real powerhouse as the products increase and as the success of the brands increases. The new churches will start to form sanctuary cities or form places in the cities that become sanctuaries, similar to gated communities in the cities.

Whole suburbs might start to become Christian owned with businesses, shops, coffee shops and restaurants. The whole community will be evangelized and brought into alignment under God, almost like their own little country.

These sanctuary cities will begin to grow, and the attitude of these Christians will be to share everything and to own everything together. Everyone will have everything in common.

Some people in these communities will have jobs in the outside world and continue to work there. However, they'll bring the money into the community so that the community can share in the finances of everyone who is working.

People that are sick might be healed, but if someone can't work for one reason or another, the community will support them. The poor will be provided for in these communities.

Christians will be known by their love in these communities. Known Christians in the community will be treated with respect and love and honor. The Christians in the community will be full of love.

Love will flow so easily that even non-Christians that come into the community will be affected by love and transformed by it, which will continue the revival.

Revival will happen in airports, coffee shops, restaurants and in taxis. Wherever these people go, they will carry a walking revival.

Everyone in the congregation will be on fire for God. They won't be cold but will be hot in their zeal for the Lord. Everyone in the community will love God and serve and love each other.

The community products and businesses will have fair wages and prices with godly values. Their brands will take off. The brands will skyrocket through these corporate communities of churches.

As churches grow all around the world, the business people in the church will link up strategically with churches in other countries.

Workers in all of the factories and other businesses will all be Christians. Because of that, fair wages and the profits will go back to the community. The wages will be competitive, and the products will be of a high value. Greed won't be an issue, and shareholders won't try to extort money from customers. The business won't look for ways to make products as cheaply as possible so that they can make the most money.

The wages at the company will be fair along with the prices to the customer. Each of the companies will have godly values. Because of that, the brands will take off.

The brands will become so successful that they will put pressure on ungodly companies. Other companies that are in the world will start to lose market share, and profits will drop from the business explosion in these churches. The global community will be very upset with these brands and with the churches.

As the brands grow and succeed and as they put pressure on the financial markets of the world with their inventions, the world's businesses will put pressure on the government. The government will elect an antichrist to come in and take away the dollar and bring in the mark of the beast.

No one will be able to sell or trade without the mark of the beast. Of course, by that time, the people who live in the sanctuary cities will have their own produce, inventions and properties, and everything will be owned by the community.

Satan will try to attack the communities, but God will supernaturally look after the Christians there with angels and protect the people who live there. The people who moved to those communities as they were led by the Holy Spirit will be protected and sustained by God until the end of time.

I have seen this vision multiple times over the past few years, and I really believe it.

Of course, a few things must happen before this vision comes to pass. First of all, churches will need to break out in revival. Many prophecies have confirmed that this will happen.

Next, churches and Christians will have to have a real desire to get back to and re-establish the book of Acts. They will need to live in community with all things in common.

If people just continue to own their own houses and live in separate parts of the city and if they refuse to move to the same area or to a gated community together, this idea won't work. If Christians were not in one place when satan attacked, it would be very hard for the Lord to protect a whole community of people unless the people were actually living in community.

These things will take time. Teachings and prophets will need to inform people about what is happening. They will provide an understanding of what it means to let go and become separate from the world and live for God and his purposes. They will need to have faith in God to sell their houses and move to a community until Jesus comes back again.

People will need faith and assurance that their pastor has their best interests at heart. They will need faith in God that he will look after them if they give up their life savings and move to a community that is shared and owned by people in common.

A book that talks a little bit about this sort of community was written by a friend of mine, called, "The Kingdom at Rose Rock" (Faith Living, Mitch's Publishing, 2015). If you'd like to find out about what it might look like for a community to operate like this, you might want to read that book.

Confirmation from Michael Bacon on Facebook (date unknown), shared with his permission

I was in the process of editing this book when a good friend and prophet, Michael Bacon, posted a video on Facebook. I was led by the Holy Spirit to watch it, and as I listened, I found that his message was similar and confirming to this message about the last day's church. I wanted to include it to confirm that the Lord is not just speaking to me about the church coming together like they did in the book of Acts. Here are Michael's words, with the meaning left entirely intact and edited only for grammatical correctness:

Good morning, Saints. The Holy Spirit has been talking to me since last night. It is time to appear at church, but I just couldn't get this out of my spirit. I want to go ahead and share what God put in my heart to release to the Body of Christ this morning.

Since last night, I've been in the spirit, praying. To be honest with you, over the last couple of days, the Lord's just been talking to me about where we broke fellowship with him and where we need to get right in our fellowship with him. He's been downloading these things into my spirit.

Last night, I had dreams and visions and different things were happening to me. The word that I woke up to this morning in my spirit was the word "interdependency."

When I woke up and heard this word, I said, "Lord, what in the world are you trying to say? Why are you giving me this one word, interdependency?" At the end, he talked to me.

I am going to be sharing this word this morning here at Glory Tabernacle Church. He told me, "Interdependency is the opposite of being independent."

I'll say that again. "Interdependency is the opposite of being independent." He showed me by the Spirit that we are entering a time right now where he is returning the church to a place of interdependency, a place where we depend on one another instead of walking independently.

In fact, he told me this morning to say this. We are about to see another Acts Chapter 2 church come back into existence. We are about to see a transformation in the church in this lifetime that we've never seen before.

In fact, when you look around, and you see all of the different denominations and the different types of churches that are around the world, there is very little unity or agreement. We are not walking in one accord, according to the Word of God.

This morning, the Holy Spirit showed me this. "Again, I am going to bring another Acts Chapter 2 experience to the church. I am going to bring the churches to a place where they can be in one accord. I am going to bring the churches to a place where they no longer act independently, but they are walking according to my Spirit and in one accord."

In fact, God is about to transform the church. Like I said, "like we've never seen in this lifetime." God is about to do something so powerful. When you go back to Acts Chapter 2, and you read about how they came together in one accord, and you read about how they waited in the upper room, they waited on God together. When they waited on God together, the power of the Holy Spirit showed up and showed out. Signs, wonders and miracles were the norm in the church. Salvations were normal in the church. Daily, the church was being added to.

I want to say that the key is this. I want you to get to the place where you realize that you can no longer be independent. You can no longer walk by yourself. I know we are at a time right now where people love independence because it is really a goal that some people pursue or chase after.

But let me tell you something: independence in our society is also tied to the root of rebellion, which is to say that you are not under anyone's authority.

God showed me by the spirit that there is a spirit of rebellion in the land. One of the reasons we need to have interdependence and to be together in one accord is because he is breaking the spirit of rebellion off the church.

We are under the authority of both Jesus and the Father. We don't do anything unless we first see the Father in heaven doing it.

That means that we have to wait on God for instructions and wait on him to show us what we need to do in this hour. Then, we need to pursue it with all of our might. We need to do it together in one accord.

Again, the word this morning is that we are to be "interdependent," not independent.

Let me ask you this morning. Are you walking in one accord with God? Are you part of the Body of Christ and are you walking hand in hand with one another? Are you there for your brother when they fall? Are you there to help love, support and encourage?

I tell you, the Lord also says that "iron sharpens iron." The Lord showed me something in the spirit about that as well. He said, "I want you to think about iron sharpening iron." He says the first thing that happens when you take a piece of iron, and you sharpen another piece of iron is that you have friction. Once you have friction, you also have heat. And once you have heat, you also have sparks.

I am going to tell you that there will be some friction and some heat. Some sparks will generate in our fellowship. Yes, some of that will be kind of rough to deal with at times. But you know what? Think about the powerful side of that comment or statement. Think about how the power of the Holy Spirit also could be created through that friction that sparks from one another.

First, we will be perfected by that friction. We will also be empowered by the heat. Amen. We are going to be empowered by the sparks of the Holy Spirit.

God is doing something.

"Iron sharpens iron." Hebrews 10:25 says do not forsake the assembling of yourselves together because we are supposed to be in the house of God. We are supposed to be there to encourage one another.

Come be a piece of iron that can sharpen another piece of iron. Amen.

Find your place. Get in one accord. Begin to seek the destiny, the purpose that God has for your life.

I tell you that time is running out. But I am telling you that God showed me that he is raising up another Acts Chapter 2 church right now in this hour — a church that will be on fire for God and that will move in signs and wonders and miracles, a church that will pursue God with all of their might.

God is about to move. I am telling you, God is going to take this spirit of independence and turn it into a spirit of interdependence where we need each other and where we realize that we can't do it by ourselves any longer. We need one another.

God bless you, and I hope the word touched your heart this morning. Amen.

Chapter 4 — The 144,000

Many people have preached on the 144,000. The Jehovah's Witnesses believe that only 144,000 people are going to heaven. They say that the rest of mankind will go to sleep and then be awakened to rule on earth with Jesus.

Certain cults and some groups of believers believe that they are part of 144,000.

Many people preach a pre-tribulation rapture and that Christians will leave the earth. They say that will suddenly say that people will realize that Christians were right about the rapture, and more people who were left behind will give their lives to God. Some teachers will share that a group of 144,000 Jews from the 12 tribes of Israel will preach the Gospel to the world because the 12 tribes were mentioned in Revelation 7.

They believe that the 144,000 will be Jews and that these Jews will take the Gospel to the world. People have many differing opinions about the 144,000 people.

First of all, I personally don't believe that the 144,000 people are Jews. I believe that this number is simply a representation of those who will be used during this time. I think that **every single person who wants to be used** in a complete capacity for Jesus to spread revival globally **will be used.**

I believe that this number is just figurative. For example, the New Jerusalem was 144,000 cubits. Revelation 3:12, speaking of the church of Philadelphia, says, "He that overcomes, I will make him a pillar in the temple of my God, and he shall go out no more. I will write on in the name of my God and the name of the city of my God, the new Jerusalem, which comes down out of heaven. And I write on him a new name."

I feel that this group of 144,000 people will be made like pillars of the Lord, pillars of the temple. Revelation 14:4 tells us, "These are the ones who were not defiled by women, for they are virgins. They are the ones who follow the Lamb wherever he goes. These were redeemed from among men, being the first fruits to God and to the Lamb."

These first fruits, these are the closest ones, the ones that follow the Lamb wherever he goes. They are like the pillars in the temple. In Revelation 21, the New Jerusalem is said to be 144,000 cubits. This measurement of 144,000 compares with the number of people who will be pillars in the temple.

The New Jerusalem is a type of person who is the first fruits of the Lord. These 144,000 people are focused on serving the Lord.

Again, this verse says, "These are ones who were not defiled by women for they are virgins. They're the ones who follow the Lamb wherever he goes. They were redeemed among men, being first fruits to God and to the Lamb."

I believe that the 144,000 are totally sold out to God. I don't personally believe that they have to be virgins as in those who have never had sex before. I could be wrong, but I personally believe that these 144,000 will be millions of people grouped together. For the sake of simplicity, I just use the term 144,000.

This group will consist of eight to 10 million people that will be used in the last days with power and signs and wonders. They will carry revival.

I believe that the reference to them as virgins means that they are set apart and have kept themselves unspotted from the world (James 1:27). They have decided to come out of the world and not be part of it.

Of course, we discussed the end time church in the last chapter and discussed that the new church will form communities that will have everything in common.

I feel that people that are set apart and that want to serve God wholeheartedly is a type of people who don't place a high priority on money or a lot of value on the things of the world.

Like virgins, these people will be set apart. The lust of the world and the lust of everything that's involved in the world will have no part of them so that it won't consume them. Their virginity represents that they are set apart.

One key ingredient in holiness is to have a life that is set apart for God — a life focused on pleasing God, with your time, energy, possessions and your money.

People who live a set apart life don't have an iPad just for work or for games, but they have an iPad that they use to minister to other people. These people who live a set apart life don't just have a smart phone for phone calls and social media; they have a smart phone that is often used to encourage people and to do ministry. These people who live a set apart life don't just have a house that is furnished nicely. Their house is not only their castle, but it a place where they can entertain strangers and homeless people and use the warmth and comfort to bring love and peace into another life.

People who are set apart don't spend extra money on great clothes to look good. They dress to have influence and not to affect the world but to draw the world closer to God. People who are set apart don't buy luxury cars, no matter how much money they have. They have a better use for their money that will bless other people. People who are set apart don't have to set time each day to focus on God and be one with him. They commune with him throughout the day, and all of their time and their life are focused on God.

People who are set apart don't look to get caught up in the latest fad that is capturing the world's interest. They are most often ahead of the curve and doing things that the world might emulate. People who are set apart don't have an issue giving $200 to a stranger or $500 to a ministry or more than 10 percent to their church each week. People who are set apart realize that all their money comes from God, and they steward the money that is allotted to them.

People who are set apart are most often deep and become frustrated when people are talking about sports and TV shows 10 minutes after the church service ends before they have even left the sanctuary. People who are set apart are led by the Holy Spirit and are directed by Jesus and the Father, and they please God all the time. People that are set apart walk in the favor of God.

People that are set apart aren't not worried about the rapture or what's happening in the world but are about God's business, doing what they are born and purposed to do. People that are set apart go about doing what God places on their heart instead of worrying about what other people are doing.

People that are set apart don't do what is popular or what the world craves, but they are following God with all they do and say. People that are set apart are hungry for the ways of God, and God is always teaching them and filling them.

People that are set apart only make up about 1 percent of the church, yet the future revival will be led by them. They are mostly unknown and not popular in the world's standards, but God knows that they will be available when he needs to use them,

I believe all of these people are not defiled by the world but are instead moved by the Holy Spirit.

Revelation 14:4 confirms this: "These are the ones who were not defiled with women, they are virgins. They are the ones who follow the Lamb wherever he goes. These were redeemed[a] from among men, being firstfruits to God and to the Lamb."

I assume that these 144,000, which is millions of people, will be directed by the Holy Spirit and by Jesus himself.

Jesus often gives many commands; he tells me to do certain things. I am led by the Holy Spirit, and he works in the background, telling me or instructing and inspiring me about what to say and do.

However, Jesus also works in my life. He directs me to write a certain book or to give money to a homeless person. He impresses upon me to approach a certain person with a prophetic word. Jesus mostly directs me, and I do what he tells me to do.

However, the Holy Spirit is working in the background in between the times when Jesus tells me what to do.

The 144,000 is actually a group of millions of people that will be directed wholly by the Lord Jesus and by the Holy Spirit. They'll be sold out to God. They won't have one foot in the world and one foot with Christ, but they'll be totally directed by Jesus and completely sold out to him.

As I said before, just because the tribes are listed in Revelation 7, I don't necessarily believe that these 144,000 will be all Jews. I tend to think that the actual names of the tribes represent functions in the Body of Christ and in the new church.

Some of the tribes might represent groups of the following: apostles, prophets, evangelists, pastors, teachers, worship leaders, musicians, writers, business owners and intercessors. That's a total of 10 groups, and you could easily add another couple of groups to that.

When the tribulation is happening and the beast is rounding up people in an attempt to destroy them and attack Christians and close down the Christian church, the communities of Christians in the new church that we covered in the last chapter will be safe and protected by angels.

Other groups of apostles, prophets and other ministries might also be active. These groups of people will go out together and minister in churches. They will reach out to people on the street and evangelize others and bring them back to the community.

As I said, all over the world, millions of people will be represented by these 144,000. Millions of people will take the Gospel to the streets and bring the message of Christ to people who are not in the community. They will go out and rescue Christians and direct them back to their community and take them to their safe haven.

Christians who are outside of the community who are starving to death or having trouble living and who are being hunted down will be saved as they cry out to God. The Lord will hear their cries. These 144,000 will hit the streets, sharing the Gospel and the love of Jesus. They will round up those people and bring them back to their communities where they will be safe.

I believe that the 144,000 will be integral to the end times. They will be serving in ministry long before the brands and products take off and threaten the world's brands. They will be operating in ministry long before the mark of the beast is enforced in the world because the world's brands are threatened.

I believe that these 144,000 — represented by millions of people — will be travelling from revival church to revival church, birthing revival. They will travel from a revival church to ordinary churches, preaching the Gospel and bringing the ordinary churches into revival. Revival churches in each city will pool resources at the peak and will book stadiums and save thousands of people.

Revival isn't just a job for the two witnesses. The two witnesses can't go to every building or every church in a nation and preach the Gospel and share the love of Jesus with people. The two witnesses will be limited in what they can do.

However, the millions of people represented by the 144,000 can travel to many churches and impact others and bring in the people that will represent the Body of Christ.

I'm not saying that if people don't join the revival church, the new church, that they aren't part of the Body of Christ. Many people who are Christians and who are sincere won't hear the messages of the prophets of the end time church. Many people won't hear the message and will stay outside of the communities.

These people are loved by the Lord as well, and he will try and protect them. However, I feel that many people's lives will be lost when the mark of the beast is released.

The antichrist will round up people and try to kill them. I'm not fearful of the antichrist or of the mark of the beast simply because I know in those times, I'll be part of a community. I believe that I4'll also be part of the group of 144,000 that comes out of the communities and preaches the gospel.

Some of the 144,000 will be captured and martyred. They'll be hated for the sake of the Lord.

As I mentioned in the first chapter, the glory of the Lord will be seen on people. The 144,000 or the millions that they represent will shine like the sun.

At certain times, they will go out of the community and walk down the street and be shining. This will attract many people and draw crowds. These 144,000 will be able to preach a message that brings people from the outside world into their home communities and the safe zones.

The people of the world will know the meaning of this radiance of faces. They will understand that the people whose faces shine are these special people on assignment from God. They will watch for them and recognize the glow when they see it. Many lost and desperate people will want to be kept safe from satan and the antichrist.

Many of these people will be watching for the shining ones to come alongside. They will then follow the radiant ones. Many people who are shining will be given gifts by others who just want to bless them and be healed by them. This will be like when Peter walked down the road, and people brought the sick out to be healed with his shadow.

These 144,000 will have amazing gifts of healing and abilities and will demonstrate the gospel with signs and wonders. Many people will be touched by them and brought into the Kingdom and brought into the safety of the communities.

These communities are protected by angels and supported and sustained by God. Anything lacking in these communities, such as food or water, will be supplied by God, likely via his angels.

It will serve people well to read a book like this so that they understand the purpose of the communities. People have made similar efforts in the past. A church called "The Church of Philadelphia" exists as well. People have tried to raise up these communities before. However, although they had good intentions, they planted these communities 50 or 100 years too soon.

I pray that this information has enlightened you. I feel that every person that wants to be used as a revivalist or an evangelist will be used as one in these last days. Jesus will need workers who preach the gospel and share with people, demonstrating with signs and wonders following. I believe that God will allow everyone who wants to be part and who is set apart, like I've explained, to be involved.

And certainly, if you're called to do that, you'll have a calling on your life. When you hear this message, it will excite you. I hope that this has blessed and encouraged you. If so, please write to me and let me know what you think of it.

Closing Thoughts

In summary, I don't believe that the two witnesses will be here any time in the next 10 to 15 years. I know that it will take some years before churches start to break out in revival and for churches to come together to form communities. I know that more people need to teach on this and share this vision for the end time church so that people can have some confidence that this is truly what God wants to happen. I sense that when revival starts to break out and when you start to see those churches form alliances, then you will know that the end is drawing close.

The two witnesses will be real people and not the Old and New Testaments like some people say they are. Everyone in the world will know them. They will be aligned with many of the revival churches, and they will help many people. When the two witnesses are here, many communities will already be established. It will be a very dangerous time for you to be a Christian if you are not already part of one of the communities.

As time goes on and we grow closer to the day, you will see that I am not the only one that has had this vision of the end time church and what the two witnesses will do and the roles of the 144,000. Look for more information on these topics and ponder what I have said in your heart for the future.

God bless you.

Thank you for purchasing my book and for supporting me.

I'd love to hear from you.

One way that you can bless me as a writer is by writing an honest and candid review of my book on Amazon. I always read the reviews of my books, and I would love to hear what you have to say about this one.

Since I read a lot of books, I always make sure to read the reviews of any books before I buy them. You can easily make a good decision about a book when you have read enough honest reviews from readers. One good way to make sure this book sells well and to give me positive feedback is to write a review for me. It doesn't cost you a thing but helps me and the future readers of this book enormously.

To sow into my book-writing ministry, read my blog or to request your own personal prophecy or life coaching from me, you can visit http://personal-prophecy-today.com. All of your gifts will go toward the books that I write and self-publish.

To write to me about this book, please feel free to contact me at my personal email address at survivors.sanctuary@gmail.com.

You can also friend request me at Facebook at Matthew Robert Payne. Please send me a message if we have no friends in common as a lot of scammers friend request me.

You can also do me a huge favor by sharing this book on your Facebook as an enjoyable book to read. This will help me and other readers.

Other books by Matthew Robert Payne

The Parables of Jesus Made Simple
The Prophetic Supernatural Experience
Prophetic Evangelism Made Simple
Your Identity in Christ
His Redeeming Love- A Memoir
Writing and Self-Publishing Christian Nonfiction
Coping with your Pain and Suffering
Living for Eternity
Jesus Speaking Today
Great Cloud of Witnesses Speak
My Radical Encounters with Angels
Finding Intimacy with Jesus Made Simple
My Radical Encounters with Angels- Book Two
A Beginner's Guide to the Prophetic
Michael Jackson Speaks from Heaven
Conversations with God: Book 1
7 keys to Intimacy with Jesus

Coming Soon

Influencing Your World for Christ
Conversations with God: Book II

You can find my published books on my Amazon author page here:
http://tinyurl.com/jq3h893

About the Author

Matthew was raised in a Baptist church and was led to the Lord at the tender age of 8. Matthew has known some pain and darkness in his life, which has led him to have a deep compassion and love for all people.

Today, he runs two Facebook groups, "Open Heavens and Intimacy with Jesus" and "Prophetic Training Group." Matthew has a commission from the Lord to train up prophets and to mentor people in the Christian faith. He does this by ministering to people through his groups and by writing relevant books on the Christian faith.

God has commissioned him to write 50 books in his life, and he spends his days earning the money to self-publish and fulfill that plan. You can support him in his ministry by donating money at http://personal-prophecy-today.com or by requesting your own personal prophecy or life coaching.

It is Matthew's prayer that this book has blessed you, and he hopes that it will lead you into a deeper and more relevant relationship with God.

www.ingramcontent.com/pod-product-compliance
Lightning Source LLC
Chambersburg PA
CBHW052111070526
44584CB00017B/2436